Sea's of Rissa

A Journey of Me

*A collection of poems by
Author Marissa Ann*

Copyright 2018 Marissa Ann

All rights reserved. Without limiting the rights under copyright above, no part of this publication or any part of this series may be reproduced without the prior written permission of both the copyright owner and the above publisher of this book.

This book is a work of fiction. The names, characters, brands, and incidents are either the product of the author's imagination or are used fictitiously. The author acknowledges the trademark status and owners of various products and locations referenced in this work of fiction, which may have been used without permission. The publication or use of these trademarks is not authorized, associated with or sponsored by the trademark owners. This book is licensed for your personal enjoyment only. This book may not be re-sold or given away to other people.

Warning:
Credits:
Cover Design by: Francessca's PR & Designs
Editor: Rachel Goldman
Blurb: Melissa Mitchell

ASIN:
ISBN-13: 978-0-578-89275-3

Author's Note
     The poems you find in this collection are various works that I have written over the years. I have always found writing to be therapeutic. My thoughts, feelings and emotions have always influenced my written words.

Some of these were written while I went through some of the worst times of my life and others during the greatest moments. Not even my novels are safe from the influence of my emotions.

The date in each title, is the date that each one was written. They are not in any particular order.

Dedication:
I'd like to dedicate this to anyone who has not always had it easy in life. Your family life, love life, career life, or anything else, can not break who you are. Hold your head high and reach for the galaxy. You can make it.

My Best-friend-(October, 2015)

I can hear the waves sometimes when I lay down to sleep.
The sea salt smell being carried on the wind.
I hear your voice calling me in.
My heart wishes to give in,
Just to see your face again.

To see your eyes shining with the love,
That only the soul of a best friend can still send from above.

I know that we will meet again.
When my life has reached its final end.
Just wait for me there,
My friend.

(Dedicated to Jessica Marie Harris 1981-2015. I will carry you with me forever my sweet Jarie.)

The Highway-(January 3, 2019)

Eighteen gears is what he likes.
Tall stick shifts and a lot of lights.
Traveling fast across the land.
In the rain, in the snow
Or across the desert sands.

Looking for the next load.
For when payday comes,
He will send it home.
He looks on the load boards,
Thinking just one more time.
Before I head home to the woman that is mine.

He sees that the bills are paid.
Thinking he's giving her all that she desires.
But the one thing she is desperate for,
Is more than a handful of hours.

She's at home right now,
Completely alone at the midnight hour.
Her heart slowly dying,
Like a wilted wild flower.

How long will she last?
Nobody really knows.
Will she hold on for dear life,
While feeling completely alone?
Or will she tell him she's had enough,
Before her heart turns to stone?

There's no doubt about the love they feel for each other.
But a relationship requires more to brighten that wilted wild flower.

She knows her love is strong,
But that highway holds all the power.
Calling to him,
In her last desperate hour.

God's Flower-(2005)

Little yellow flower shining so brightly.
I wish you would shine year round for me.
Never dying or aging,
Just looking brilliantly.

Little yellow flowers are sent from God, you see.
To remind us that He is watching, oh so carefully.
So when you see the little yellow flowers,
Reaching up to Heaven, you'll see.

That it's a tiny reminder from God,
Saying, "Please Remember Me".

Angel Wings-(March 17, 2014)

Let me sleep unto the night.
Like a joyous beginning at the end of thine life.
Tempt not to awaken me
And do not fear my flight.
I know it feels like the end,
But it really is just the beginning.

So go ye out unto the world.
And find thy love, thy passion and thy joy.
Know that ye were loved by me.

Always watch the roads ahead.
And when hard decisions come to pass and hold
Thee captive in the crossroads of life,
Know that I am with thee still.
Like two hearts forged together with iron strings,
I will always be there with thee on Angel Wings.

Home-(March 24, 2014)

I'm tired of the struggles life throws at me.
It gave me my soulmate,
But put him in a place too far from me.

My heart feels like it's breaking,
Every time I remember his goodbye.
Even though I have hope it's not forever.
My sun no longer shines.

We have been two souls separated by distance and time.
But we will forever be one heart combined.

So I sit and watch the days slowly die.
Waiting for that special time,
The clouds no longer cover my sky.

And once again the sun will begin to shine.
To lead my soul home,
Where two hearts combine.

Winter Love (2018)

Snowflakes falling from the sky.
The air chilling you and I.

Gazes locking across the fire.
Both unsure of this desire.

Our voices carry on the wind.
Then our hands touch and a sizzle begins.

It starts deep within our soul,
Taking over complete control.

Never letting the two of us go.
Loving you more than gold.

I will forever follow you in the cold.
Until the end when we are old.

Mother's Light-(2016)

The beginnings of a heart breaking,
Never seen with the naked eye.
The silence is overwhelming,
But there's a raging storm inside.

When the heart is weeping,
You can hear it in a sigh.
Listen closely my child,
For the light is fading from your mother's eyes.

Do you still remember when,
She sang to you a lullaby?
Her world was you
And you alone.

For years she struggled,
So you'd have something of your own.
She wasn't perfect,
But she made you a home.

The years have slowly passed.
Now her heart is shattered like glass.
You can hear it in her sigh.
Trust me son,
For the light is quickly fading from your mother's eyes.

Momma's Man-(January, 2017)

The day you were born I looked at you.
Little pink, scrunched up face
Hazel eyes with a hint of blue.
I never knew what love was until I saw you.

I said, "You'll grow strong in this life I make for you. Never give up because that's not what a man should do. Live your life and let your light shine through. I'm so happy God gave me you.

Six years old, first day of school.
You said, "Mommy I don't need you to hold my hand. I need to do this like a man."

I said, "You're growing stronger in this life I'm making for you. Never give up because that's not what a man should do. Live your life and let your light shine through. I'm so happy God gave me you.

Twelve years old with a football and blood on your chin, you said, "Momma I don't need you to hold my hand. I can take a hit like any man."

I said, "You're growing stronger in this life I made for you. Never give up because that's not what a man should do. Live your life and let your light shine through. I'm so happy God gave me you.

Fifteen years old with a basketball in hand, you said, "Momma I don't need you to hold my hand. I'm going to perfect this jump shot like a man."

I said, "You're growing stronger in this life I made for you. Never give up because that's not what a man should do. Live your life and let your light shine through. I'm so happy God gave me you.

Seventeen years old with a contract and a silly grin, you said, "Momma I don't need you to hold my hand. I'm joining the Army to be a better man."

I said, "You're growing stronger in this life I made for you. Never give up because that's not what a man should do. Live your life and let your light shine through. I'm so happy God gave me you.

Nineteen years old, graduation day with a full fledged smile you said to me, "Momma I don't need you to hold my hand. Because of you, your baby boy is now a man."

I said, "You've grown strong in this life I gave to you. You'll never give up because that's not what a man would do. Continue to live your life, letting your light shine through. I'm so happy God gave me you."

What To Do-(December 14, 2000)

I don't know what's going on when my heart starts to flutter.
When you're in sight, my heart is filled with fright.
I don't know when this thing started or when it'll stop.
How can I keep on going without you breaking my heart?
I'm so confused about what to do.
I can't think straight.
All I think about is you.

Never Ending-(January 4, 2019)

I walked away years ago,
Hoping life could just move on.
But my heart wouldn't let go.
The days turned into months,
The months into years.
In the dark of night,
I would dry my tears.
While memories flowed across my mind.
Thoughts of the time that you were mine,
Protected my heart through the darkest of hours.
No bruise, or cut
Nor even the fires.
Could extinguish the flames,
Of my deepest desires.
To feel the lightning,
That only you could inspire.
Sparking my soul to fly even higher.
I walked the longest road through hell.
Two decades later, I find you well.
Now I lay safe in your arms that never fail.
While you whisper softly,
"I'll love you always and keep you well."

Confused-(2000)

My knees start to shake when you're in sight.
My heart is filled with wonder,
My mind with fright.

When will this feeling stop?
When did it start?
How can I listen to my mind,
Without breaking my heart?

I'm so confused.
What should I do?
I can't think of anything,
Except for you.

Should I ignore you?
Or just give it time?
I can't think straight.
My heart controls my mind!

Lost-(2014)

Crowded by people yet so alone.
Wishing they could see more deeply,
Past the mask that is all for show.
Asking yourself why don't they see me?
Maybe they don't really want to know.
Always crying in the darkness,
Behind the shadows of despair.
Waiting for a family,
That doesn't really care.

Alone (January 2020)

Her eyes weren't made for crying.
Although you seem not to care.
For they fill and leak daily.
As if she were full of despair.

They used to shine like amber in the sun.
So full of life and love that she shared.
Her heart freely given,
Broken in pieces but repaired.

No her eyes weren't made for crying.
Although you seem not to care.
For they are dulled by the sadness
She tries to hide with her shield.

Her soul can't beat the darkness,
That you have now put there.
Over shadowing the brightness,
Extinguished like a flame.

Her eyes most certainly weren't made for crying.
Although you seem not to care.
That she hides behind a mask,
While she feels all alone.

Things You Say (2019)

You call me names,
I can't quite ignore.
They hurt me deeply,
Down to my core.

The sweet phrases given so rarely,
Are not enough to heal the aching sore.
Your words more powerful than fists of stone.
They bury themselves deep within the soul.

Dimming the light that my eyes have shone.
I'm oh so weary of being alone.
And the sadness I feel even when you are home.

Can you not be sweet once more?
Like the man I used to adore.
You need to stop being a fool
Before I walk out that door.

The Dance (2013)

I see your eyes,
They are so Blue.
Oh what a sigh I do.

Your kiss tasted so right,
I'll always remember this night.
Closing my eyes, I still see you.

Smell your scent,
It surrounds the room.
We're going to make this love come true.

I'll always be in love with you.
So, Hold my hand as we dance around the room!

You Left Me (2010)

Your words were so cold.
Ever so bold.

You never cared!
We didn't have anything rare!

Now I cry.
Do you even wonder why?

I don't see that you do!
I loved you so!

You turned away to go!
I thought we were gold!

I'll grieve.
But I'll get over you leaving me!

Things We Knew (May 2010)

What we thought we knew, made us try.
I really didn't want to say goodbye!

There was so much still left to say.
Even as I watched you walk away.
I still pleaded for you to stay.

I figured our love would always last.
Now I know we are in the past.

My heart is now on the mend.
If only we could have known then!
How all of this would end.

Friends Til The End (April 2011)

I seen your fears,
Through the tears.
Felt the pain from your heart.
Why did we part?

I cried a lot, while you were gone.
Felt as if I couldn't carry on.
Why did you have to go,
And hurt me so?

Now you are looking for a way back in.
Asking if we can be friends again.
I don't know why, You are so surprised.

By my reply.
Friends until the end.
That was back then!

Time Everlasting (April 2018)

We looked at each other,
You seen my tears,
As we stood here.
You touched my face,
In that special way.
I heard you say,
You would always love me this way.
I knew it was true.
The whispered sweet words from you.
I know in my heart,
We'll never be apart!
We embrace,
Every day.
Dreams of us,
All the while.
You take my hand,
You make me smile.
A white dress,
Down the aisle.
Some day, we will find...
That our love,
Will outlast time!

In The Mists of Time (2013)

You kissed my cheek,
Sparking a need.
I held my breath,
But you weren't through yet.

Your mouth met mine,
In this mist of time.
I close my eyes
And sigh deep from inside.

Time goes by.
Your hand forever in mine.
Our hair turning gray.
Our love stays the same.

I am yours,
You are mine.
My dream come true,
In the mists of time.

Loving You (Dec. 2009)

Love from you, from the start.
You know you have my heart!

Your kiss is sweet upon my lips.
Everything our love is...

You spoke words so sincere.
Makes me wish you were here!

I see the stars in the sky.
They make me sigh..

We held each other tight.
Embrace with all our might.

The world is better now that you're here!
Makes me cry sweet tears.

Love from you from my heart!
Never to be apart!

Run To Me (Nov. 2009)

Run to me!
My arms are opened wide.
I don't have to tell you.
You know I am always on your side!

Your tears are real.
We will deal.
Trust in me.
You'll always feel.

This love I give,
Freely to you.
Will always be,
Waiting for you.

Time stand still!
At least for me.
I smile now,
As you run to me!

Letters Of Love (September 2009)

I am writing these letters of love,
Because you are the one I dream of.
I think of your face,
In every single place.

The world we know,
Will never show.
That it is ours to share.
As long as you meet me there.

Your kisses are mine!
When we meet in this time.
You are my man!
I'll show you what I can!

You are my delight,
In the middle of every night.
Heaven above,
Will lead us to love!

Gone Awhile (Oct. 2009)

You came to me.
All I could see,
Was my heart beating fast.
I thought we would last.

All the kisses we shared.
Made me think that you cared!
Holding me close.
I thought we had chosen.

The tears came on slowly.
I thought you wouldn't leave me lonely.
We could have been happy.
Like we were back then.

The way we touched.
Made me fall so much!
I wish I could smile.
But you've been gone for awhile!

Walking As One (2009)

We walk as one.
Our lives have begun!
I could see,
You smiling at me.

When we touch at night,
We love with all our might!
Kisses we share,
Let me know that you are there.

The way I feel in my heart,
Makes me believe we will never part.
I am your wife.
We will walk as one in this life.

When our passion ignites,
We hold each other tight.
Showing our love,
Until we pass to the above.

Sunshine (2009)

The sun shined today,
When you came home to stay.
I was so glad,
To no longer be sad!

Our spoken words of love.
You are all I have ever dreamed of!
We cried in each other's arms.
You said you were enraptured by my charms.

A love this sweet,
Every time we meet.
Can not be thrown,
Away like an old stone!

There's only you for me,
And me for you.
As we always knew,
This is true!

Sweet Voices (Jan. 2010)

I let your words,
Melt my heart.
Because you said,
We would never part!

The look in your eyes,
Made me start to cry.
I thought our love was true!
Did you not feel it too?

Your kiss was sweet.
I thought it made me complete.
There were so many choices!
Listen now to our own voices!

Down That Broken Road (May 2018)

We hold each other tight.
Embracing with all our might!
The world is ours to share.
I knew you'd always be there.

Our time went slowly by.
In your arms I know why.
The way we touched is not new.
You know I will always love you!

The tears that fell.
As we got to know each other well.
The pain of our pasts,
Wasn't meant to last.

Now we are together again!
Just like we were back then!
I knew you wouldn't go.
Forever away down that broken road!

First Taste of Love (Dec. 19, 2020)

I remember when,
We were so young.
Our lives had just begun.
But I loved you then!

Twenty years passed.
It wasn't that long.
Now we are strong.
So we've been told.

You still mean,
The whole world to me.
I will never forget,
The first taste of love with thee.

Where Are You Now (Nov. 2009)

We were young but we still thought we knew,
How we felt, didn't you?
We were told not to grow up too fast.
They said we wouldn't last.

Remember the times we shared?
It makes me sad to think again.
Of the dreams about us from back then.

You said we would meet,
Again one day.
I hoped it were true.
Did you?

The tears I cried, they were real.
Didn't you know how I feel?
I would have begged for a chance for us back then.
I know that I will see you again.

I Saw You There (Nov. 2009)

I saw you there.
Couldn't stop my stare.
Your eyes met mine.
We lost all sense of time.

You spoke so sweet.
Made me feel more complete.
I cried for you.
You know it's true.

Your hands holding mine.
The sweetness of you,
Making me need you.

We will touch even more.
Of this, I am completely sure!
You really cared.
When I saw you there!

Heartbeat (2009)

The way we always touch,
Makes me love you so very much!
All the tenderness from you,
Shows that it is true!

You always hold me close.
Don't you want to know,
That in my dreams I see,
How very real it seems.

Our kisses are always sweet,
Every time we meet.
Our pain is gone now.
We made each other better somehow.

You've made me complete.
With every heartbeat!

Broken Hearts (2009)

Remember when you made me cry?
Could you not tell me why?
You thought we'd be free.
Can't you see what you did to me?

When did I ever hurt you?
You hurt me too!
My tears are real!
Don't you know how I feel?

The world was our's to share.
I really thought you cared!
But now I see,
You never really loved me!

I believe in a second chance.
We had a sweet romance!
I don't want us to be apart.
Can't we heal our broken hearts?

The Fear Is Gone (2009)

It was sad the day you broke my heart.
I really thought we'd never part.
The tears falling down my face,
Was proof it's not supposed to be this way.

Why did you leave me so?
I'm so hurt, can't you see?
We were supposed to be for eternity.
When we touched, it was real!

Didn't you know how I feel?
Why can't we try once more?
I still love you!
That's for sure!

Kiss me again, just once more.
Remember when you were mine?
Together we could carry on.
Until the fear is gone.

Soft Whispers (May 2010)

Soft whispers so light,
Can't you hear me in the night?
Just to hear the words,
Makes you feel so sure.

Delicate and sweet.
My voice repeats.
You know I mean what I say.
Each and every single day.

The tears won't come,
Because I know.
The lullaby I speak,
Will make you more complete.

So close your eyes now.
No more cries now.
Listen as mother speaks.
Soft whispers to make you complete.

God's Sweet Kiss (May 2010)

A touch of spring,
A brand new start.
Love with all your heart.
The blossoms are small,
Soft to the touch.
We've missed the sun,
Oh so much.

Makes us happy,
To see it again.
Like it always did back then.
The warmth of it,
Gives us smiles.
If only for a little while.

The tenderness of God's sweet kiss.
The dew and the mist.
It can always be like this.
Heaven on Earth,
Full of bliss!

Everything is brand new.
We can see it, Me and you.
We look around just once more.
Heaven bound for eternity or more!

That Night (Nov. 2011)

You were hurt.
I could see.
There was so much more to say.
Why did it have to be this way?

You held me close.
I held you.
This is hard.
We've come so far!

We had so much!
Now we don't have a choice.
The end is near,
Just as we feared.

We can see all that we shared.
You promised to always be there.
Neither of us know what to do.
You can feel it too.

We needed each other.
Holding tight.
We almost loved again this night!

Dancing Slow (Nov. 2011)

In your arms,
I turn towards you.
You can feel this passion too.
Moving as one through our hearts.
Never to be far apart!

Your touch is sweet.
It means so much to me.
You're on my mind every single day.
You know it to be true.
Every night too.

We kiss.
Your mouth on mine.
We feel this bond.
It makes me cry.
You see the tears in my eyes.

You wipe them away.
There's nothing to really say.
Your lips move over mine.
Igniting a flame.
Dancing slow in this sweet glow.

Hang In There (2014)

Life's not just a journey,
It's an adventure.

Some hang with it,
Despite the dangers.

Others are sidetracked,
By the small features.

Although the rewards are greater,
If you hang on for the big picture!

Beaches (2014)

I need sunshine and beaches,
With a few margarita mixes.

Throw in good friends and good times,
And you'll never hear me bitchin'!

Love On The Wind (Jan. 10, 2016)

I used to love you way back when.
Though the love was fleeting and like the wind.
It was too big, I never could have held it in.

So I released it,
Letting it fly!
Though it stayed with me throughout all time!

Lying dormant under the ice that was once my heart.
Waiting for you to come back,
Before I break apart.

One Heart (Jan. 2010)

We were one heart,
From the very start.

Just one kiss,
We never did miss.

We have found such bliss!

Wonder why we both sigh.
Together we have cried.

Do you know?
I love you so!

Years together, It's still brand new!
It will always be me for you!

One heart glows,
For us alone.

Love For You (2015)

Loving you from the start.
You've always known you held my heart.

You were the greatest,
Even when we were miles apart.

You spoke words so sincere.
I wish now you were here!

Every time I see the stars in the sky..
I just sigh..

Wishing we could hold each other tight.
Embrace each other with all our might!

The world was better when you were here.
Now I am full of fear.

Love for you comes out as tears.
This is all I'll have for the rest of my years.

Those Words (2001)

The words were low,
Please don't go!
I begged you then,
Do you remember when?

You cried with me,
But I couldn't make you see.
The tears still come now.
I wish I didn't remember somehow.

Why did you go?
I really want to know.
Wish you could see.
What this has done to me.

The tears still come in the night.
I try to fight.
This pain so real!
Do you still not know how I feel?

You Brought Me (2003)

You brought me through the dark.
I want to be where you are.

You brought me through the storms.
Kept me safe and warm.

You brought the sunshine too.
My tears fell slow.

We seen sad days.
But you brought me through anyway.

I don't have to think about the past.
You brought me joy at last.

We hold each other tight.
Through the darkest night.

You brought me,
And I brought you.

Our love is true.
Because God gave me to you!

Mark Your Love (2003)

I saw your eyes that night.
It all felt so right.
Your gaze meeting mine.
We lost sense of time.

The way you smiled at me.
I could see...
How you felt by your words.
I'm very sure...

I felt your hands touching mine.
So slow.
I wanted you to know.

That I longed for your kiss.
Sweet as this...
The way you spoke.
So soft to me.

Mark your love.
Speak from your heart.
I hope we never part.

You do as well.
I can tell.
The way your eyes look in mine.
You stop time.

As we dance,
This sweet romance.
I hear you whisper.

Mark your love!
Make me your own!
We both know,
I will go!

With you in your dreams.
It must seem..
Holding each other close.
It's so...

Breathing each breathe with you.
My heart beats fast too.
I hope for another kiss.
Like this..

Your handsome face I see.
You make me smile.
For longer than a while.

The sound of your voice is so low.
You know where I want to go.
I catch my breath again.
You whisper like you did then.

Mark your love my sweet darling.
Before I kiss you,
And we lose this moment.

A Tryst In Love (2018)

Do you remember how we looked in each other's eyes?
I cried..
Seeing your face, in that place.
Hearing your voice,
I so enjoyed.
Our time together when we first met,
Could be better yet.

Because our feelings have grown from that day,
To something like love...
I must say...
A tryst in love from the start,
When we gave each others heart.

Time has gone by.
A place remains for you and I.
As we watch the years go by.
I'll whisper words so low and true.
Because I know you love me too.
A tryst in love will do.

Passion's Call (2011)

We embraced.
Breathing hard.
I know where you are!
That last kiss, making me want more.
You know it for sure.

The dew between us is so sweet.
You don't know what you are doing to me!
You whisper my name.
Another kiss.
Nothing compares quite like this.

You took me.
I gave it all.
I'm amazed by it all.
The stars danced, we drifted off.
Our passions called!!

We Walked Away (2011)

We walked away.
It was hard to take.
A very sad day.
Why did it have to be this way?

Your tears were mine.
We both still cried.
It was harder this time.

Look at me again!
Like you did way back when!
Can you see it through my eyes?
Don't let our love die!
I'll try harder this time.

When you hear my voice,
You'll know I made my choice.
You feel me with such joy.
Oh what a sad, sad day.
Because we walked away!!

Never The Same (August 2011)

Our love has just begun.
As we breathe together as one.
Gasps sounding in the night.
This can only be right.

Holding me tight within your arms.
Telling me just who you are.
The heat between us is so pure.
Twisted together on that bed.
Words left unsaid.

Swirled together in delight.
Held each other throughout the night.
Kissing again and again.
Making it better than.

Sparks setting us aflame.
I know I'll never be the same.

Whisper You Want Me (2000)

I close my eyes, I still see your face.
There's more than just a trace.
Of passion in our kiss.
Nothing could taste as sweet as this!

You tell me you love me,
So perfectly.
I need you to see,
Just what you do to me.

The fire in your touch.
Needing you so much.
I see in your eyes,
Where the passion lies.

You sweep me into your arms.
I know how perfect for me you are.
Loving and sweet.
These things you do to me!

Moving real slow.
This will never get old.
Hearing you whisper you want me.

Your Eyes (2000)

You looked at me and I smiled.
It didn't take a while.
That handsome face I gazed into.
I knew our love would be true.

The sweetness you showed me.
Made me so happy.
Always there.
I could see how much you cared.

The way you looked.
Your eyes on mine.
You were ready this time.
To say you are mine!

You took me by surprise.
When I looked into your eyes.

Sparks At Night (2020)

When you said my name,
I knew I'd never be the same.
Always making me smile.
It's been that way this whole while.

Sparks at night,
From your touch.
I love you so damn much!
There's a heat,
Between you and me.

Holding me close.
Don't you know?
We can see the stars.
I know where we are!

Dancing through life with you,
You feel this way too.
I know it's true.
When you whisper,
You love me.

Walking To You (2012)

We both looked.
That's all it took.
Me in your arms,
Seeing the stars.

You're special to me.
Kiss so sweet.
The faintest touch.
Makes me want you so much!

Feeling you breath,
Sweet ecstasy.
Is what I feel when you make love to me.

All the pleasure's of,
These dreams at night.
You know it's true.
I smile as I'm walking to you.

Take My Fears (2006)

I work so hard,
And try so much.
But I don't know,
If I am loved.

The pain is real,
It feels too great.
I want to rip,
It out somehow.

We've known for a while,
What's going on.
I know I need,
To be strong!

I cry so much.
You see my tears.
Hold me again!
Take away my fears!

What We See (2007)

When I look at you,
I see the love.
I know that I am the one you dream of.

When we walk hand in hand,
I see your smile.
We've been together,
For quite a while.

What we see,
When you look at me,
Is more than just you and me.

I cry so much when we are apart.
We hold each other's heart.
Sweet delight in your arms,
I always want to be where you are.

When we are alone,
I feel your touch.
Loving each other,
Oh so much.

What we see,
When you look at me,
Is more than just you and me.

A love that will last.
Through all time.
We will never say goodbye!

Heartstopping Kisses (2018)

I closed my eyes and smiled.
I sighed..
Your face I saw in my mind.
You pressed your mouth to mine,
I was more ready this time.
You knew it too,
I could only ever love you.
The sparkle streams from the sky.
Shining down on you and I.
Feeling your arms holding me close.
Your heartstopping kisses are mine to know.
Your caress, so soft and sweet.
Make me feel so complete.
Hearing your voice calling my name,
I will never be the same.
You take my hand, holding it tight.
I shall never forget this night.
I cry the tears you wipe away.
Only true love could feel this way.
The sparkle streams from the sky.
Shining down on you and I.
Feeling your arms holding me close.
Your heartstopping kisses are mine to know.
You give me one more,
I'm holding my breath.
You aren't through quite yet.
We've bonded together, you and me.
Heartstopping kisses for eternity.

Walking In Our Dreams (2014)

I close my eyes as you whisper my name.
I'll never be the same.

The way you look at me,
I can see...

All the love pouring from your heart.
We shall never be apart.

Your kiss tells me,
Everything that's true.

I hear the sound,
Your laugh making me smile.

The taste of another kiss,
On my lips.

My heart beating fast.
Take a chance with you.

I take a breath,
I sigh with you.

I know you're walking in our dreams too.

Cherished Love (2013)

I wanted to hold you close.
Don't you know?
That's why I reached for you,
On that night.
I smiled as you kissed my cheek.
I could see...
The way you were looking at me then,
As you took my hand.
You'll always be in my heart,
Because you are...
The only one,
I dream about.
I will give sweetness only to you.
Because you feel like I do.
What we share is more than love.
You know what I'm speaking of.
The taste of your kiss upon my mouth.
There's no wonder how,
We found love in these moments of...
Your touch...
Your caress...
You know the rest!
The wonders of love.
Hearts beating fast.
Our love is for...
Cherishing love better than before!

I want to thank everyone who has supported me but most especially my husband. He has been a rock for me since this journey in my life began. I couldn't do this without your unwavering support. I love you so very much!!!

Other Titles by Marissa Ann

Wolfsbane Ridge MC Series

Book 1 Timber's Fairy
https://books2read.com/u/47lz7E

Book 2 Blade's Pixie
https://books2read.com/u/38RPla

New Year New Me Anthology featuring Chucky's Pride, A Night Howler's MC Story
https://books2read.com/u/mdnwOX

A Call Of Magic Limited Edition
https://books2read.com/callofmagic

www.ingramcontent.com/pod-product-compliance
Lightning Source LLC
Chambersburg PA
CBHW051411290426
44108CB00015B/2240